First Facts®

ANCIENT EGYPT

CLEOPATRA

BY **JANEEN R. ADIL**

Consultant:
Leo Depuydt
Professor, Department of Egyptology and
Ancient Western Asian Studies
Brown University
Providence, Rhode Island

Capstone
press®

Mankato, Minnesota

First Facts are published by Capstone Press,
151 Good Counsel Drive, P.O. Box 669, Mankato, Minnesota 56002.
www.capstonepress.com

Library of Congress Cataloging-in-Publication Data
Adil, Janeen R.
    Cleopatra / by Janeen R. Adil.
    p. cm. — (First facts. Ancient Egypt)
    Summary: "Describes the life of Cleopatra, including her rise to power and death" — Provided by publisher.
    Includes bibliographical references and index.
    ISBN-13: 978-1-4296-1936-3 (hardcover)
    ISBN-10: 1-4296-1936-8 (hardcover)
    1. Cleopatra, Queen of Egypt, d. 30 B.C. — Juvenile literature. 2. Queens — Egypt — Biography —
Juvenile literature. I. Title. II. Series.
DT92.7.A35 2009
932'.021092 — dc22   2008000271

Editorial Credits
Christine Peterson, editor; Alison Thiele, designer; Wanda Winch, photo researcher; Marcy Morin, page 21,
    project production

Essential content terms are **bold** and are defined at the bottom of the page where they first appear.

1 2 3 4 5 6 13 12 11 10 09 08

TABLE OF CONTENTS

EGYPT'S LAST QUEEN

Cleopatra VII was the last queen of ancient Egypt. She ruled from 51 BC to 30 BC. As queen, Cleopatra was charming and smart. She also wanted to keep her power at any cost.

Cleopatra was famous around the world. She is still famous today. Yet, parts of her life remain a mystery.

ANCIENT EGYPT

The time in history called ancient Egypt began around 3000 BC, about 5,000 years ago. It ended in 30 BC, when Rome took over Egypt.

DISCOVER!

No one knows what Cleopatra really looked like. She is often shown with dark hair. Some paintings show her with blonde hair and light skin.

BECOMING A QUEEN

Cleopatra was born in 69 BC. Her father, Ptolemy XII, was **pharaoh** of Egypt. In 51 BC, Cleopatra's father died. She and her younger brother, Ptolemy XIII, now ruled Egypt.

Cleopatra's brother wanted to control the country. Fearing Ptolemy may kill her, Cleopatra fled to Syria. There she gathered an army to fight for the throne.

pharaoh: a king in ancient Egypt

DISCOVER!

In ancient Egypt, a queen could not rule without a king. Cleopatra shared power with her brothers or her oldest son.

Fight for the Throne

Roman **emperor** Julius Caesar came to Egypt to stop the war. Rome wanted Egypt's riches, and Cleopatra needed Caesar's help. She had to sneak into the palace to meet with him.

In 48 BC, Caesar made Cleopatra queen and her brother king. But war broke out between Ptolemy XIII and Caesar. Ptolemy was killed. Cleopatra now controlled Egypt.

emperor: a man who controls several countries

DISCOVER!

To get past palace guards, a friend hid Cleopatra in a rug.

Life with Caesar

Caesar stayed with Cleopatra in Egypt for about nine months. In 47 BC, he returned to Rome. A few months later, Cleopatra had a son. She named him Ptolemy Caesar. Julius Caesar may have been his father.

In 46 BC, Cleopatra and her son went to Rome. Two years later, Caesar was killed. Cleopatra and her son returned to Egypt.

Discover!

Cleopatra was the only member of the Ptolemy family who learned to speak Egyptian. The rest of her family spoke only Greek.

ANTHONY AND CLEOPATRA

By 42 BC, Mark Anthony ruled the eastern half of the Roman **empire**. Cleopatra knew Rome could be a powerful friend to Egypt.

In 41 BC, Cleopatra traveled to Rome. She wanted to show off her riches and power. She dressed like a goddess. She rode a golden **barge** with purple sails.

barge: a large, flat ship

empire: a group of countries with the same ruler

DISCOVER!

Greek historian Plutarch wrote the *Life of Anthony* about AD 75. His book gives some of the best information about Cleopatra.

A Life of Luxury

Anthony and Cleopatra fell in love. They lived in Cleopatra's grand palace in Alexandria. In time, they had three children.

As rulers, the couple had many **luxuries**. They hosted feasts and parties. They had jewels, gold, and other riches.

luxury: something you don't need but is enjoyable to own

DISCOVER!

Legend says that Cleopatra once dissolved a pearl in a cup of wine and drank it.

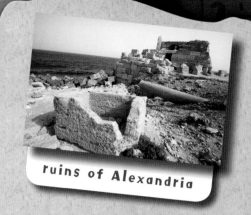

ruins of Alexandria

THE CITY OF ALEXANDRIA

Alexandria, Cleopatra's beautiful city, was the most famous seaport of its time. It stood on the banks of the Mediterranean Sea. The great Pharos lighthouse kept watch over the city. At that time, the royal palace was the world's richest building. Today, only a few ruins are left.

ruin: pieces of a building that was destroyed long ago

BATTLE FOR POWER

A Roman leader named Octavian wanted Anthony's power. He said Cleopatra wanted to take over Rome. People turned against her.

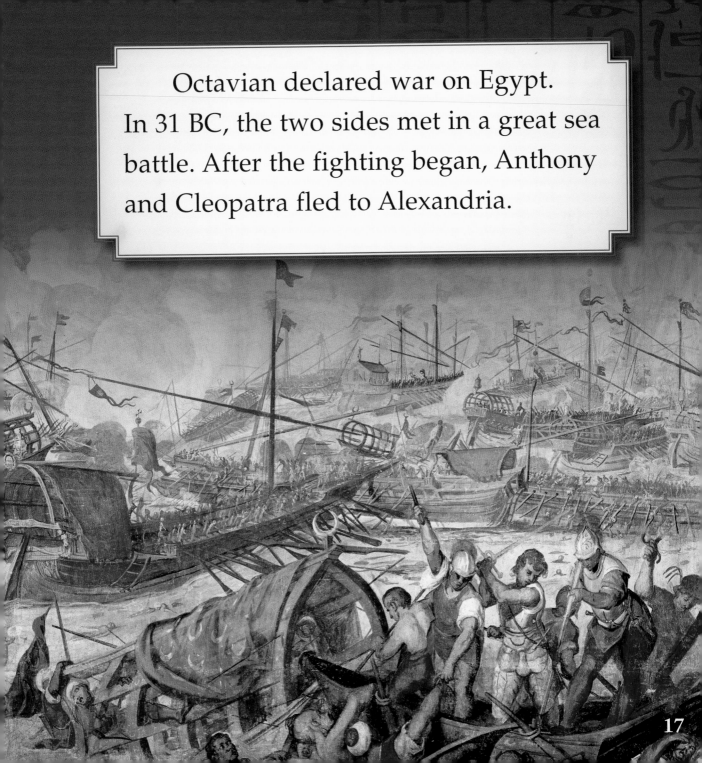

Octavian declared war on Egypt. In 31 BC, the two sides met in a great sea battle. After the fighting began, Anthony and Cleopatra fled to Alexandria.

END OF AN EMPIRE

Octavian captured Alexandria in 30 BC. Anthony believed Cleopatra was dead and killed himself. But Cleopatra was still alive. She feared returning to Rome as a prisoner. Legend says Cleopatra let a poisonous **asp** bite her and soon died.

Cleopatra ruled Egypt for 21 years. She gained riches and fame but lost Egypt to Rome. She remains one of the most famous rulers in history.

asp: a poisonous snake

Cleopatra's life may be famous, but her death is a mystery. Many historians believe she killed herself by letting a poisonous snake bite her. Others say she hid poison in a hollow comb she wore in her hair. Some historians say Octavian may have killed Cleopatra.

HANDS ON: EGYPTIAN CROWN

In ancient Egypt, both men and women wore jewelry. Cleopatra's jewelry was made from gold, jewels, and brightly colored stones. Make your own crown to feel like Egyptian royalty.

What You Need

- scissors
- thin cardboard
- fabric paint, any color
- gold spray paint
- glue
- jewels, beads, sequins
- tape or staples

What You Do

1. Cut a strip of cardboard about 2 inches (5 centimeters) wide. It should be long enough to wrap around your head and overlap 1 or 2 inches (2.5 or 5 centimeters).

2. Lay the cardboard flat. Use the fabric paint to decorate your crown with Egyptian designs or other patterns.

3. When the fabric paint is dry, spray the whole crown with gold paint.

4. Glue the jewels, beads, or sequins to the edge of the crown.

5. Tape or staple the ends together to finish your crown.

Glossary

asp (ASP) — a small, poisonous snake

barge (BARJ) — a large, flat ship used to transport goods

emperor (EM-puhr-uhr) — a man who rules a group of countries

empire (EM-pyr) — a group of countries that have the same ruler

luxury (LUHK-shuh-ree) — something that is not needed but enjoyable to have

pharaoh (FAIR-oh) — a king of ancient Egypt

ruins (ROO-ins) — the remains of a building or other things that have fallen down or been destroyed

READ MORE

Adams, Michelle Medlock. *The Life and Times of Cleopatra.* Biography from Ancient Civilizations. Hockessin, Del.: Mitchell Lane, 2005.

Benduhn, Tea. *Ancient Egypt.* Life Long Ago. Milwaukee: Weekly Reader Early Learning Library, 2007.

Miller, Ron, and Sommer Browning. *Cleopatra.* Ancient World Leaders. New York: Chelsea House, 2008.

INTERNET SITES

FactHound offers a safe, fun way to find Internet sites related to this book. All of the sites on FactHound have been researched by our staff.

Here's how:
1. Visit *www.facthound.com*
2. Choose your grade level.
3. Type in this book ID **1429619368** for age-appropriate sites. You may also browse subjects by clicking on letters, or by clicking on pictures and words.
4. Click on the **Fetch It** button.

FactHound will fetch the best sites for you!

Index